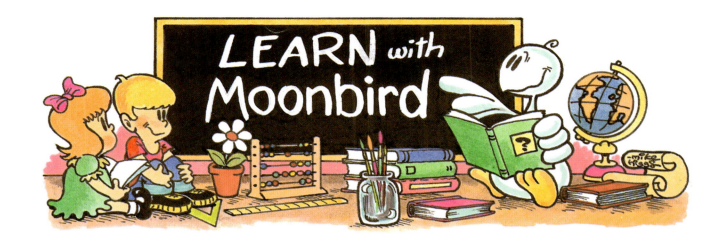

safety in school

Illustrated by Mike Higgs

Written by Sally McNulty

Published by Rourke Enterprises, Inc., P.O. Box 3328, Vero Beach, Florida 32964. Copyright © 1984 by Rourke Enterprises, Inc. All copyrights reserved. No part of this book may be reproduced in any form without written permission from the publisher. Printed in the United States of America.

Library of Congress Cataloging in Publication Data

Higgs, Mike, 1945-
  Safety in school.

  (Learn with Moonbird)
  Summary: Moonbird helps schoolchildren understand safety rules on the way to school, in the classroom, and on the playground.
  [1. Safety education—Juvenile literature.   2. Children's accidents—Prevention—Juvenile literature.   [1. Schools—Safety measures.   2. Safety.   3. Extraterrestrial beings]
I. Title.   II. Series: Higgs, Mike, 1945-   Learn with Moonbird.
LB3407.H53   1984   372.17′7   84-6883
ISBN 0-86592-721-9

ROURKE ENTERPRISES, INC.
Vero Beach, Florida 32964

Wicked Willie Wasp lives on a noisy planet. His family and friends buzz, buzz, buzz, all day long. Everywhere you look, there are wasp nests. Nobody wants to visit.

Wicked Willie was lost, far from home. As he flew through space, he saw the planet Earth. "I will visit Earth today," Wicked Willie thought to himself. "I can make lots of trouble for everyone."

As Willie was thinking his wicked thoughts, the Mouse children were getting ready for school. Their friend, Moonbird was helping. "It is a beautiful day," said Moonbird. "I will walk to school with you."

No sooner were they out the door, than Wicked Willie flew over to Mary Mouse. He buzzed a secret in her ear. This is what he said. "There is no traffic coming. You can run across the street."

Mary Mouse ran. Moonbird saw a car coming. Quickly, he picked Mary up. He flew her to safety.

"Why did you run across the street, Mary?" asked Moonbird. "You should know better. Usually, you look both ways and listen before crossing."

BEFORE CROSSING THE STREET, ALWAYS LOOK BOTH WAYS AND LISTEN. CROSS WHEN THERE ARE NO CARS COMING.

"I don't know what happened," said Mary.
"I heard a buzzing in my ear. The next
thing I knew, I was in the middle of
the street."

"I must get to the bottom of this,"
said Moonbird.
"Hee, hee, you can't catch me," said
Wicked Willie. He zoomed in a circle above
Moonbird's head.

Moonbird tried to catch him, but Willie got away. "You musn't teach children to do things that are not safe," Moonbird said to Wicked Willie. Willie just buzzed.

That day in school, everything went wrong, thanks to Willie. First he buzzed his magic buzz in Matt's ear. Matt ran down the stairs. He tripped and fell. Moonbird was too late to save him.

WHEN YOU RUN ON THE STAIRS, YOU CAN HURT YOURSELF OR OTHERS.

Willie sat on Mabel's head and buzzed.
Mabel walked over to the hamster cage.
She set the hamster free. Everyone ran
around the room, trying to catch the
hamster. The teacher stood on a chair.

Moonbird found the hamster, hiding under a desk. He put the hamster back in its cage.

BE KIND TO YOUR CLASSROOM PETS.

Harry was a goody-goody mouse. He
never broke the rules. Today, Wicked Willie
whispered in Harry's ear. "Buzz, buzz,"
he said.

Harry ran to the fire alarm. He pushed the button. Can you guess what happened?

NEVER SET OFF A FALSE ALARM. FIREMEN COULD HAVE BEEN HELPING PEOPLE AT A REAL FIRE.

The whole school went on a fire drill. The teachers were angry. "How could this happen in *our* school?" they said. Harry was upset. He knew he had done something very wrong.

UNNECESSARY FIRE DRILLS WASTE THE TIME OF TEACHERS AND STUDENTS.

Bruce was a happy mouse. He had many friends. Wicked Willie whispered in his ear. "Buzz, buzz," he said.

On the playground Bruce started pushing his friends around. "Stop," said Moonbird. "You don't really mean to do that!"

PUSHING AND SHOVING CAUSES ACCIDENTS.

Next, Wicked Willie found Abby. She was always a little forgetful. "Buzz, buzz," Willie said in Abby's ear.

Abby gave the classroom door a hard push. She wasn't thinking about who might be standing behind it. Boom! Down on the floor fell Sissy, Sarah and Sam.

ALWAYS OPEN AND CLOSE DOORS SLOWLY.

Wicked Willie whispered another secret to Matt. "Buzz, buzz," he said in Matt's ear.

Matt pulled a chair out from under Harry.
Moonbird was quick this time. He grabbed
Harry as he fell.

**FRIENDS AND TEACHERS GET ANGRY AT SILLY
TRICKS IN THE CLASSROOM.**

Willie found Mabel again. Can you guess what he said in her ear?

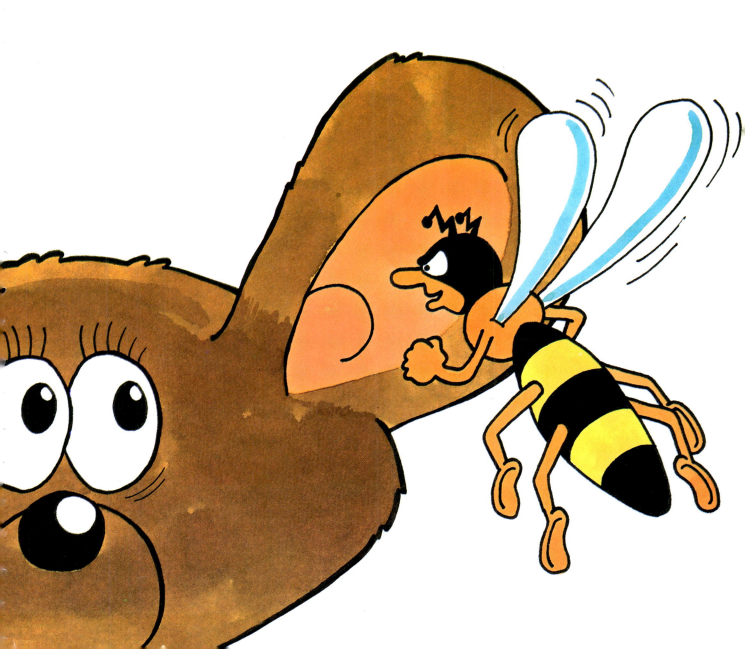

Mabel threw a sharp pencil across the room. Moonbird caught it before it hit someone.

OBJECTS THROWN IN CLASS COULD BADLY HURT SOMEONE.

Wicked Willie wasn't finished yet. He flew into the lunchroom. Bruce was eating potato chips. "Buzz, buzz," went Willie.

Bruce threw some potato chips at Sam.
Sam threw his straw back at Bruce.
"Stop it at once!" said the teacher.

"This has gone too far," thought Moonbird. "I must do something about that wicked wasp."

Moonbird thought and thought. He looked over at the class fish tank. A fish net was lying nearby. "Maybe I can catch Wicked Willie with the net," he said.

Willie had found Mary again. "Buzz," he said. Slam went Moonbird with the fish net! "Bzzzzzzz," said an angry Willie.

"I've got you now," said Moonbird. "I am going to put you in a magic space bubble. You will be sent back to your own planet. I don't ever want to see you again!"

"Whew," said Moonbird. "Thank goodness he's gone. Now we can all get back to being ourselves again."

WHAT IF A STRANGER ASKS YOU FOR HELP?

You have often been told not to take rides from strangers. You already know never to take candy from strangers.

What would you do if a stranger asks you to help look for his lost dog? What if he asks for some other kind of help?

Do not go with the stranger. Tell him you will find a teacher or parent to help him. Leave quickly. Find an adult to help.